A Bit of a Leftie

Dave Puller

A Bit of a Leftie

ISBN 978-0-9567733-1-9

Published by
Puller Publications
58 Orchard Road West
Northenden
Manchester
M22 4ED

A CIP catalogue record of this book can be obtained from the British Library.

Book designed by Michael Walsh at
The Better Book Company
5 Lime Close, Chichester PO19 6SW

Printed by
ImprintDigital.net
Seychelles Farm, Upton Pyne, Exeter Devon EX5 5HY

Contents

This book is dedicated to all the people I love,
those who are living and those who are not.

I also wish to thank Babs, Cher, Kristian, Liz
and Amelie for their love and support. Amelie
tells me my poetry doesn't rhyme, but she likes it anyway.

Thanks to Claire Mooney for all her years
of encouragement, organising and gigging
with me, often in very trying circumstances.

A special mention to three friends who work at Tesco,
Barbara, Elaine and Val. Not fans of
poetry they came to watch a gig Claire had
organised in Levenshulme. They loved the night and have
been fans ever since.

LOVE ALL
HATE NONE.

Introduction

I have had many occupations in my life but performing poetry is, without doubt, the best job I have ever experienced. I like talking with my audience and hope, at the end of my performances, that they have enjoyed my poetry, and may be able to see poetry in a different light.

I started writing poetry whilst I was at school, mainly because I did not like, or enjoy, the poetry we were being taught. My poetry is direct and, I feel, questioning. I write about love, life, class, politics and all things that matter to us as human beings. I perform my work in cafes, libraries, those that have not been closed, houses, theatres, community centres, festivals and I have even done an arena gig.

In the past I have written for, and appeared on the radio, televison, and the theatre but, being honest, I have found those areas of work patronising, pretentious and classist and did not really enjoy those experiences. I did, once, when I was younger, want to be an actor, and I applied to the Manchester University School of Drama. At the audition I was asked to be an egg in a lift, a tree, put on tights and dance to the rhythm of a drum and asked what I thought of Shakespeare. At the end of the audition I was informed that the audition panel would write to me in a fortnight. The letter never arrived. My acting career was stopped in its tracks.

My poetry is not to everyone's liking but I do hope you find something in my book that you can relate to, and that, above all, you enjoy reading the poetry.

I have been supported, unconditionally, in my poetic endeavours by my long suffering family. They put up with my rants, my politics and my regular campaigns without complaint.

If you enjoy the poems in this book and you would like me to perform at a venue you can contact me on the following numbers.

01616131577 ~ 07815006671
e-mail d.puller@ntlworld.com.

Dave Puller

Join the Army

I grew in Wythenshawe, a large and wonderful council estate in South Manchester, and like many council estates it is a working class area full of good people, many of whom have been let down by the political classes. We have a central shopping precinct called Civic Centre and every now and again the armed forces roll up with their recruiting paraphernalia, in an attempt to get the local youngsters to join up.

Now, there are not many killers in Wythenshawe, and I am sure the people who join the armed forces don't think of themselves as killers, but that is what armed forces do. They kill our perceived enemies, in the name of our country. Most people who join just want a job or career and this may be the only option open to them.

This particular time the Army came calling and ran a competition. They wanted a new recruiting slogan. The winner would get a ride in a tank, be allowed to fire a rifle and go on a weekend camp with the Army. The competition was only open to 15 to 18 year olds. I lied about my age and entered. It went like this.

We can give you a uniform
We can make you look smart
We can put fire in your belly
We can put stone in your heart

We can teach you to drive
We can teach you to run

We can give you a tank
We can give you a gun

We can teach you to swim
We can teach you to drill
But best of all
We can teach you to
KILL.

It didn't win.

Local Hero

Growing up in the 50s and 60s I wanted to be like all the heroes I read about in comics and saw on television. I was just like any other child, with their dreams, hopes and ambitions. Some younger people may never have heard of the characters in this poem, but then I suppose we all have our own heroes, heroes linked with our childhood.

I wanted to be Flint McColough
Leading a wagon train
I wanted to be The Lone Ranger
Riding across the plain
I wanted to be Flash Gordon
Roaming through outer space
I wanted to be the great Alf Tupper
Winning another race
I wanted to be Robin Hood
Feeding all the poor
I wanted to be Desperate Dan
Walking through a door

I wanted to be Denis the Menace
Walking his dog Gnasher
I wanted to be Roy of the Rovers
Scoring with a smasher
I wanted to be a poor kid
Living down on Bash Street
I wanted to knock Lord Snooty

Off his palatial seat
I wanted to be Popeye
Winning Olives' hand
I wanted to be Chief Sitting Bull
Making his last stand

I wanted to be a goodie
Doing the baddies down
I wanted to drive a stagecoach
Bringing food into the town
I wanted to do all those things
That children dream about
But somewhere along the way
The child got lost
The adult got out.
And the heroes ran away.

You Are

As I approached my 50th birthday in 2001, my friend Jan was diagnosed with a terminal illness, cancer of the Oesophagus. Jan had gone to live with her daughter and they decided to throw a birthday for me at the house. On the afternoon of my birthday, with my friends Claire Mooney, Chris, Helen, my partner Babs and a couple of other of Jans friends we met at her bedside.

Claire sang some songs, I performed some poems and, although Jan was very ill, it was a wonderful and uplifting experience. Towards the end of the afternoon Jan became very tired and we realised it was time to leave her. As I sat on the bed next to Jan we hugged each other and said how much our friendship had meant. She asked if I would compose a poem for her funeral. I kissed her and said goodbye. She died a few days later.

I wrote two poems for her funeral, one called "The Essence of Jan" and another called "You Are".

I have never performed the first poem, other than at Jan's funeral. The second poem I now perform regularly. It is one of my favourite poems and I hope it has a certain relevance for everyone.

You are my cup of tea
You are hot
You are my favourite biscuit
You are my umbrella in the rain
My shade from the hot sun

In spring you are my walk by the river
In winter you are my warm fire
You are my smile when I am sad
My lift when I am down

You are my most delicious ice cream
You are my happiest dream
You are my light in the dark
You are my playground in the park

You are my sight
You are my breath

You are my friend
You are my lover
You are my father
You are my mother
You are my son
You are my daughter
You are my sister
You are my brother

You are everyone
I have ever loved
You are
Just You.

England Always Wins

In September 2011 there were riots in many cities throughout England, including my own city Manchester. The political elites trotted out all their usual clichés about what caused these riots.

They were caused, they said, without a hint of irony, by mindless thugs and hooligan intent on destroying our society. I wrote this to satire the politicians' reaction to those riots.

The riots left me wondering what sort of society turns out people who's' sole objective was to get their hands on a pair of overpriced trainers which were manufactured in the sweatshops of the Far East.

Whilst the angry
Burned and looted
And the poor emptied bins
None of us should worry
Because England always wins

Whilst the rich hid and sheltered
And tax cheats stroked
Their chins
None of us should worry
Because England always wins

Whilst single mothers were insulted
And the youth blamed for their sins

None of us should worry
Because England always wins

Whilst the poor still freeze in winter
And charities shake their tins
None of us should worry
Because England Always wins

So whilst some sing
Rule Brittanie
And the privileged hide their grins
None of us should worry
Because England always wins.

Help for Heroes (or killers)

In 2011 I read an article that said the charity Help for Heroes was the biggest receiver of public donations, dwarfing the donations received by most other charities. Help for Heroes was set up to help injured and traumatised armed forces personnel upon their return from duty.

Now forgive me for being pedantic or cynical but I believe that if our government sees fit to send our armed forces to kill foreigners, because they are deemed to be our enemy, then the least it can do is look after them if they return home injured, or look after their families if they are killed whilst on duty.

We should remember that every war our country has been involved in since 1999 has been an aggressive one, that is to say that we have done the invading. But the military and government propaganda machine continues unabated with injured military personnel wheeled out at major sporting events to be applauded as though they were performing seals .People have asked me if this is an anti-war poem. I suppose it is.

Join us in the Army
You can be the best
Make yourself a killer
That's better than the rest
You'll make lots of friends
Have your own community
You can kill men, women and children

With impunity
You can join the Navy
Or become a Royal Marine
You can fire your missiles
From a nuclear submarine
You'll make lots of friends
Have your own community
You can kill men, women and children
With impunity

What about the RAF
Fly your own Tornado plane
You can drop bombs on civilians
Kill, burn and maim

You will all return as heroes
In Navy, Blue or Green
You've defended our democracy
Served your country
And your Queen

We'll all be very proud of you
We'll wave our flags and say
It's three cheers for our heroes

HIP
HIP

Tunnel of Love

When I was fourteen I went out with a girl from school. I thought I loved her, but at fourteen you think you love every girl you know. In the summer of 1965 she finished with me and I was devastated.

On our estate there was a youth club and every summer they organised a trip to Blackpool for the local kids .My ex girl friend said she would go back with me, just for the trip .As you can guess I was delighted, overjoyed, excited, and very naïve.

As we boarded the coach, the youth workers gave us three pieces of fruit, an apple, an orange, and a banana and we promptly threw them at pedestrians, out of the open windows, as the coach sped along the road .It was a great trip and this poem came out of that day .It is a favourite poem of mine.

That day in
The tunnel of Love
She kissed me to
Perfection
That day in
The tunnel of Love
She
Eased my juvenile erection
That day in
The tunnel of Love
In the warm
Blackpool weather

That day in
The tunnel of Love
We rocked our bodies together
That day in
The tunnel of Love
I'll remember
For evermore
That day in
The tunnel of Love
Two poor kids
From Wythenshawe.

The day after the trip I called round to the girls' house, she told me to go away and that she really had only gone back with me for the day trip. I felt humiliated.

Further humiliation was heaped on me many years later when I was shopping at our local Civic Centre and I noticed her in one of the shops. I went over to her and asked her how she was. She pretended she did not know me and walked away.

However, when I read this poem at my performances I repay the compliment with a little twist at the end.

QANA
(MK-84 Guided Bomb BSU-37B)

In April 1996 the Israeli Air Force, in one of its periodic and murderous onslaughts of Lebanon, attacked a UN compound in the town of Qana, slaughtering defenceless men, women and children. The Israelis had told people living near to the compound to leave their homes and seek shelter there. The People, naturally, believed they were safe .The Israeli attackers obviously thought otherwise. Over a 100 people were said to have been murdered by the attack.

At first the Israelis, supported by their American backers denied they were responsible for the atrocity. This was obvious nonsense and a brave and brilliant writer working for The Independent newspaper, Robert Fisk, a ferocious seeker of the truth, went into the compound and found remains of a shell used in the attack. It had an American serial number on it and that number is part of the title of this poem.

Neither the Israelis, nor the Americans have ever issued an apology for the massacre and ten years later the Israeli Air Force launched another attack on the town of Qana.

Qana
Where Jesus
Turned
Water
Into Wine

And
Where
The Israeli
Air Force
Turned
Men
Women
And Children
Into
Dust
Courtesy of
The
USA made
MK-84
BSU-37-B
Guided Bomb.

As I write this book of poetry in 2015 the Israeli armed forces are still bombing and killing Palestinian men, women and children.

We are Special

In March of 2012 the Conservative British Prime Minister David Cameron visited America and spoke at the White House. Standing next to President Barack Obama he defined the supposed special relationship between America and Britain. He used the examples of violence and war, listing the conflicts at which the two countries had stood side by side. I feel if a relationship is defined by violence there is something seriously wrong with it. I wrote this poem after listening to the Cameron speech.

He used the analogy of war
To denote their friendship
A friendship
Cloaked in blood
They stood together
Their special partnership
Wrapped around the souls
Of women and children
From Napalm,
Phosphorous
To Cluster bombs and drones
Invasion after invasion
The relationship was indeed
Special
Steeped in murder
Criminality and Guilt
They stood together
Giving us their handshake

Of Hypocrisy
Their smiles
Of deceit
Their speeches
Full of lies.

People for Sale

I read an article some time ago which reported that the human slave trade was well and truly still in business. In the Philippines, once a month the worlds biggest slave market is held. Whole families are sold, sometimes together, sometimes not. When I read the article I wondered what the sales patter of the auctioneer might sound like.

Come on
What will you give me
For this one
You can see
He has big muscles
Strong legs
Kick him
He has good teeth
He can work on your
Farm
In your
Factory
He has a woman too
I can show you her
Look
She is beautiful
She can clean
Your
Mansion
Cook your

Food
Care for your
Children
Or
You
Could
Just
Use
Her
For
Sex.

Labour Member of Parliament

I was once very naïve about politics, well certainly in my teens. My local Member of Parliament was a Labour MP and I believed he was a socialist. How wrong I was. This poem is about him and where he ended. It is a place where many so called working class heroes go, and it is a place that should not exist.

It was always his desire
To become a Labour MP
To fight for freedom, justice and
Democracy
To humiliate the
Tories
When they crossed
Swords
Then abolish
The House of Lords

It was always his desire
To become a Labour MP
To work for justice and
Democracy
To argue with the
Tories
When they crossed
Swords
Then work to reform
The House of Lords.

It was always his desire
To become a Labour MP
Look at things like
Democracy
Talk to the
Tories
After crossing swords
Then discuss issues with
The House of Lords

He did become a Labour MP
Forgot about
Freedom, Justice and
Democracy
Had lunch with the
Tories
Instead of crossing swords
The he retired to
The House of Lords.

Mam

This is a poem about my mother, or Mam, as she was known to my brothers and sister. She died at the age of 49, after suffering from cancer for a number of years. She had a tough life and, although not perfect, she was a wonderful and inspiring person and I loved her very much. Her death left a huge hole in the lives of all her children, me included.

As her death approached she turned to Catholicism, and, during the final weeks of her illness the local priest and nuns visited and helped her to cope with her impending death. Although I do not believe in God, they were genuinely caring, considerate, empathic and kind. They organised a quite unforgettable funeral. This poem came out of that period of my life.

Mam
If you're in
Heaven
Is it true what they say
There's no gas, electric or
Council tax to pay
No ambitious politicians
To tell you their lies
No nationalism,
No borders
Imaginary enemies to despise
No famous celebrities
No rich or poor

Nobody to mug you
As you approach your front door
No homeless beggars to avoid
In the street
No pretence
No lies
No two faced deceit
No interest free credit
No low interest loans
No
County Court bailiffs
To repossess your homes
If it's like that in heaven
I'd like to come one day
Tell me Mam
Is it true
What they say.

A Poem for Harry Patch

Until his death, on 25th July 2009, Harry Patch had been the longest surviving British serviceman. Harry died a week after Henry Allingham, another veteran who had lived through the horror of World War one.

Harry had not spoken about his experiences until he had passed his 100th birthday. He was a man full of humanity, humility and honesty and when I read his book it was evident that he viewed war as a complete breakdown of the human spirit. He stated that he did not want to kill anyone and that he only ever shot at the ankles of his perceived enemy, even when they were approaching him with a bayonet fixed to their rifles.

His statement that war was, in effect, legalised murder, should be emblazoned on the gates of the Houses of Parliament. He said war made no sense. He was correct.

Harry Patch, from
Coombe Down
Sent to meet the devil at
Passchendaele
To serve King and Country
To be part of the slaughter
To fight
To crawl past his dying friends
Like a thief and robber

Passchendaele
Where rats grew fat
Feeding on his dead comrades
Where Harry shot at the ankles of his
Declared enemy
So he wouldn't kill them
He was, he said
A semi-pacifist
He thought war made no sense
He thought war was mindless
He thought war was
LEGALISED MURDER

Harry Patch from
Coombe Down
Sent to meet the devil at
Passchendaele
The anti-war
Semi-pacifist
Rest in Peace.

Can I ask you if you vote Conservative?

In 2009 the Conservative held their conference in my city of Manchester. We were a city in lockdown.

As I approached the centre where they were holding their conference I was stopped by one of their researchers and asked if I would be voting Conservative at the next general election. I responded thus.

They gave us Thatcher
They gave us Blair
They gave us a thing called
Community care
They gave us riots
They gave us war
They locked poverty
Behind the door
They sold electric
They sold gas
They trampled on the
Working class
They broke the railways
Into bits
Destroying communities
They closed the pits
They gave us a society
Without empathy or pity
They gave the reins of our
Country

To the vipers
In the city
Who
In their Ivory towers
Sit
Steal and
Gloat
So you ask me if a
Tory will get my
Vote
My answer is
NO
NO
NO
NEVER.

Clichéd Love

Many years ago I had a friend who was always boasting about how much he loved his wife. He would talk about loving her all the time. In fact he used clichés to describe his love.

One day he came round to my house to tell me he had fallen in love with his sister-in-law. Almost at once he began using the same clichés to describe how much he loved his new love. I got the idea of this poem from him.

He worshipped the ground
She walked on
She was his
Soul-mate
He would climb mountains
For her
Cross the fiercest sea
Walk over hot coals
He'd love her forever
Or at least until he found
Someone else
To
Fall
In
Love
With.

Friendship

Although I don't perform this poem very often I think it is a poem I actually like very much. I had stopped reading it because I felt it seemed a bit soppy, and needed adding to. The idea for the poem came, initially, from a newspaper article I read about older people getting back in touch with their first loves.

One night after a performance a woman came over and told me how much she loved the poem, because she felt it was about her and a friend she had been recently reunited with. This friend was a boy she liked very much at school, but had lost touch with over the years. She met up with him again at a school reunion and they realised how much, over the intervening years, they had missed each other.

I thanked her and spoke to her for a little while and a few days later I added extra lines to the poem.

Now that we are friends
After all these years
We can share
Each others laughter
Calm each others fears

We can release the thoughts
Which
Remained inside
Our heads

Talk about things
That would have
Remained unsaid

We can touch each others
Hearts
Dry each others
Tears
Now that we are
Friends
After all
These years

We can
Kiss
We can
Love
We can
Laugh
We can
Cry
We can
Ask
Each other
Why we
Ever said
Goodbye.

Do You Want a Free Olympic Sized Rowing Lake?

After the 2012 Olympics were awarded to London, the richest school in the country (Eton) was offered in the region of £22 million pound (some estimates say it was nearer £34 million), so they could build a new rowing course, to host the Olympic rowing championships. This money was given to Eton, not lent to them. In order to avoid any criticism a new town, Eton Dorney, was invented. It does not really exist, and we were told that this new town was hosting the Olympic rowing contest. Of course we know it was Eton because we saw the Eton College Rowing Club buildings in the middle of the course. But fair play to Eton College, they had to agree to a proviso in order to get the money. This is where the poem comes in.

Enjoy yourselves
Enjoy the facility
Your new Rowing Course
Courtesy of
The Taxpayer
After all
Why would you
Need to pay for it
When
You have promised
To let poor
People use it

As
Long
As
They
Bring
Their
Own
Boats.

On Hearing the News of a Royal Pregnancy.

This poem doesn't really need an explanation, as it speaks for itself, or rather it displays my feelings towards privilege. I do accept that my views on the monarchy may be a little extreme, but I believe that there is no place for such an institution in a supposedly, classless, democratic and meritocratic society. By having a monarchy it proves that our society is not any of those things.

The whole nation
Was ordered to
Celebrate
To supplicate itself at the feet of
Privilege
To celebrate the impending arrival
Of a lifelong benefit recipient

No workless
Feckless
Tirades
Aimed at this offspring
No benefit cuts for this family
No cold winter nights
Afraid to
Warm the home

No empty bedroom tax
For this

Parasitic bunch
Just exhortation
To bend the knee
Doff the cap
And grovel
At their
Feet

And
Smile
Whilst
We Are
Doing
It

How Will You Kill Me?

I wrote this poem after reading comments from a certain Harry Windsor (also known as Prince Harry).

He had been serving in Afghanistan, as a pilot. His comment was simply that he was good with his thumbs. The comment left me with the impression that he was likening his killing of his country's supposed enemies to playing games on his computer. He had completely missed the historical context of why he was killing citizens of another country. At the end of the poem I use a quote from Hannah Arendt from her study of Totalitarianism.

Will you kill me in your gas chambers
As I sing my last breath
Then burn my body in your furnace
Will you kill me with your rifle
My life extinguished by a flick of your finger
Will you kill me with your knife
Looking into my eyes
As I take my last breath
Will you kill me with your machete
Laughing as you mutilate my body
Will you lock me in my Church
Burning me alive
And as I scream
Will your dance of Victory begin

Will you pack your vehicle with
Explosives
Driving it into my Mosque
Screaming the name of your God
As you kill me
Will you crush me with your Tank
Taking my land as your prize
Will you kill me with your Phosphorous Shells
Burning holes through my body
Will you kill me with your Landmines or
Decapitate me with your Cluster Bombs

Will you incinerate with Missiles
Fired from your plane
Will you cut off my Head
Smiling for your camera
As you do so
Will you torture me before
You kill me
Will you kill me with your
Sanctions or your blockade
Will you kill me through
Your Hate, ignorance or fear

Whichever way you choose to kill me
You have no excuses
Only dogs and children
Follow orders
You have a choice
You can kill me
Or let me
LIVE.

Sex in a Text

In February of 2015 I read an article that stated more and more couples were having sex by text. I had previously read that certain celebrities were indulging in something called tantric sex, or sex without any physical contact. I though how strange this phenomena was and wrote this little poem.

They were having sex by text
Not as noisy as the real thing
Less mess and quicker though
No embarrassing silence
At the end of the
Act
No awkward moment
Waiting to se who
Uncouples first

The whole thing lasting
No longer than
Twenty seconds

Just
Like
The
Real
Thing
She
Thought.

IDS

In 2004 Tory Ian Duncan Smith started the Centre for Social Justice. It is described as an independent think tank, established to put social justice at the heart of British politics. It is no such thing. It is an odious, vicious organisation which has been at the heart of some of the nastiest social policies introduced by the Conservatives, first with the Liberal Democrats from 2010, and after May 2015, by the Tories themselves. Its board of directors is almost wholly made up of multi-millionaire Tory supporters. At the head of this right wing think tank is Mr Ian Duncan Smith, the architect of the bedroom tax and many other anti-working class policies, designed, principally, to punish people for being poor, and to make them poorer still. Ian Duncan Smith once used the phrase "work frees people".

This poem came when I was asked to perform at an anti-bedroom tax meeting in Bolton, and write a poem specifically, for the occasion, about Mr Duncan Smith.

Displaying
All the arrogance
Of the powerfully
Insulated

He mocked those less
Fortunate
Inventing new words and phrases
To demonize them

His peevish
Spiteful
Vicious
Words

Having the desired effects
Towards
His victims

The multi-millionaire
Part-time SAS killer
Full-time
Bigot

Member of
The let's make poor people suffer
Brigade

The man from the
Centre for Social Justice

Destroying lives
Creating chaos
Smiling and
Cheering
Whilst
He
Did
So.

Ian Duncan Smith resigned as Minister for Work and Pensions on the evening of March 18th. He stated that the cuts aimed at the disabled, revealed in the budget by Gideon Osborne, were too extreme. Duncan Smith had finally developed a conscience. REALLY.

Let's Go To War
(A patriotic holiday war song)

2014 brought the 100th anniversary of the start of the slaughter that was known as the 1st World War. The jingoism the anniversary brought with it, fuelled by the press and politicians proved that, since the outbreak of that dreadful conflict, political leaders have learnt nothing from history. They always seem to be looking for a way to make themselves our new heroes, proving that they can kill our supposed enemies, after having a vote in Parliament course.

Oh come all ye faithful
We'll march you off to war
You can visit places like Verdun
The Somme
Passchendaele
And
Many
Many
More

You can sleep in trenches
With mud up to your knees
With dead comrades laid beside you
And miling rats for company

We'll give you
Patriotic songs to sing
When we send you
Over the top
Sing loud and clearly boys
Never
Never
Stop

Don't run away or try to hide
From the horror of it all
They'll arrest you for desertion
Put you up against a wall

As the firing squad prepare
To send you on your way
Remember what they told you
As you singed up for your holiday

Oh come all ye faithful
We'll march you off to war
You'll visit places like Verdun
The Somme
Passchendaele
And
Many
Many
More.

How Do You Say I Love You?

Reading an article about how many of us find it difficult to say the words, "I Love You", gave me the idea for this poem. Try it.

Do you whisper it gently
Do you shout it out loud
Do you say it together
Do you say it in a crowd

Do you say it when you are nervous
Or when you are really calm
Do you say it when you are holding hands
Or when you are arm in arm

Do you say it when you are naked
Lying on a bed
When you say it do you mean it
Or is it just something
To be said

Do you say it very often
Or once in a while
Do you say it in embarrassment
Or say it confidently
With a smile

Do you say it when you are shopping
Or driving in a car

Do you say it close together
Or say it from afar

Do you say it in an e-mail
Do you say it in a text
Do you say it watching telly
Or just after you've had sex

Do you say it on a bus
Do you say it on a train
Do you say it on a ship
Do you say it on a plane

Do you find it is something easy
Or difficult to do

There is only one way to say it

You just say

I
LOVE
YOU.

I Am a Rebel, Honestly

This is a poem about a friend of mine, a fellow poet and a supposed rebel, who accepted an honour, from his Queen.

He said that he only took the bauble because his fans urged him to.

He bent the knee
Bowed his head
Towards his
Queen

Then
As he returned to join the
Line of Sycophants
A smile crossed his
Face

A smile of
Satisfaction

He held the bauble
In his hand

No more thoughts of
Rebellion
In his
Head.

Frozen

I wrote this poem in February of 2012, when I read that Afghanistan was experiencing its worst winter in 100 years. British soldiers had taken delivery of expensive new weapons. On the streets of Kabul, over one weekend, 47 children and 12 homeless beggars had frozen to death. After the deaths, soldiers of the invading coalition had been despatched to deliver blankets to citizens of the city. The price of heating oil was so expensive that the majority of city could not afford to buy it.

As the children
Froze
The soldiers took delivery
Of their gleaming new
Weapons
As the children
Froze
The soldiers
Put
Bullets
Into their
Gleaming
New
Weapons
As the children
Froze
The soldiers
Fired at

Their
Declared
Enemy
As Fathers and
Mothers
Washed the
Lifeless bodies of
Their
Dead
Children
As
Families looked for
Warmth
The soldiers
Handed them
Blankets
Offering them their
Stare of
Contempt
And as the ground
Froze over the
Graves
Soldiers cleaned
Their
New
Weapons.

Olympic Legacy

As many of you may remember, Britain, or really London, hosted the 2012 Olympic Games. The games were a huge success and would leave a legacy that would inspire future generations, or so we were told. I remember listening to BBC Radio 5 Live, which offered an endless supply of celebrities who had, or were in the process of setting up their own charitable trusts or foundations. These celebrities served up an orgy of vacuous clichés and drivel. This poem came about after I had listened to another celebrity drone on about how much he was doing to alleviate the problems of the poor. When I perform it I try to deliver it in the tone of an un-inspirational speaker, you know the type. We have all heard them.

I have a way to inspire a generation
The unemployed the sick
The disabled
The feckless
Set up your own
Charitable Trust for
Underprivileged Children
It's all the fashion
Everyone's doing it
Olympic Medal winners
Footballers
Actors
And it is all

Tax deductable
You can hold
Charity Auctions
Where rich tax avoiders can buy
Things they don't want, or need
And claim tax relief on the tax
They don't pay
You could get an MBE
Become a Lady or a Lord
You can then sleep in the
House of Lords
And get £500 a day
So come on
You unemployed
You sick
You feckless
You disabled
Start up your own
Charitable Trust for
Underprivileged Children
What's that I hear you say
You want me to stop using
Vacuous clichés
Stop patronizing you
You want me to go away
To eff off
Before I do
I have another great idea
You'll love
This one
It's called **THE BIG SOCIETY.**

The Big Society was an idea propagated by David Cameron and his friends .Essentially it entailed the closure of government funded community services, sacking all the workers and getting volunteers to run what services were still open. What a wonderful idea.

Not a Real War Crime

In May of 2010 the Israeli government sent its Navy and Commandos into international waters to intercept a flotilla of ships that had sailed from Turkey. The ships were part of a humanitarian mission and were attempting to reach the port of Gaza. The Israeli government conducts a sea, land and air blockade on Gaza, making it, literally, the biggest prison in the world. The flotilla waa attacked and the ships boarded. On one of the ships, the Mavi Marmara 10 people were killed by the Israeli forces. It was an act of piracy, and murder.The ships were taken into the Israeli port of Ashdod and all goods on board were confiscated.

In October 2014 the International Criminal Court ruled that the action taken by the Israeli government was, in fact a war crime, but that it was not a serious enough war crime for Israel to be prosecuted. It was suspected that the American government put pressure on the ICC not to persue a court action against their friend Israel. The poem came out of this story.

It was a war crime
But only a small one
One not worth pursuing
The killers for
The victims
Unarmed
Shot on the deck of
The Mavi Marmara
Executed in their
Cabins
The injured
Imprisoned
The ship
Confiscated
Its supplies
Destroyed

No
War Crime Trial
For
The American friend
But why would there be
When they
Can do it
Again
And again
And again
And Again.

The Food Parcel

It is 2016, and in the past year the governments trusted food parcel charity The Tressell Trust has handed out 1,084,604 food parcels to people in England. These food parcels contain enough food for three days, and in order to get one you have to have an authorised, signed, piece of paper. This paper states that you are deserving of this food parcel.

Unofficial figures state that the number of food parcels given out, both by the Tressell Trust, and other charities is nearer the 3 million mark.

Tories, such as Ian Duncan Smith, David Cameron and Boris Jonson claim that the success, of the food parcel programme, shows what a wonderful, caring and compassionate country we live in. How perverse a comment?

They were lined up
All the boxes
They contained lots of tins
New potatoes
Even tinned Rhubarb
There was Pasta
Biscuits
Lots of Tesco value food

Nice of Tesco to contribute
Enough in each
Box

To last three days
Though the poor could always come back
Another two times
A sort of three strikes and
You go hungry rule

But they always needed to have
A signed piece of paper
To signify that they were entitled
To this gift
I wondered what they would do then
With no authorised
Signed piece of paper
Having already had their
Three gift boxes

Probably
Starve
Or as some have already done
Commit
Suicide.

Philanthropic Misunderstanding

I find it strange whenever I see rich people being lauded for their philanthropic endeavours. We see them on the TV, hear them on the radio, read about them in the papers, and they themselves tell us how charitable and giving they are through their twitter accounts. This short poem is about one such couple. I wrote it after the couple were awarded the title of "Philanthropists of the Year". They didn't hand the title back. Being philanthropists I thought they might have done so.

If the couple were
Such good philanthropists
Whey were they still
So
Very
Very
Wealthy
?

Peterloo

In 2009 my friend Claire Mooney and I decided to run a night, in rememberence of the Peterloo Massacre of August 16th 1819. It was on that day in 1819 that the Manchester Patriotic Union had organised a demonstration, at Petersfield, Manchester, calling for Parliamentary reform, and which was attended by 60,000 people. As Henry Hunt, a radical activist, began to speak, the Manchester Yeomanry, on orders from the Leaders of Manchester rode into the crowd. Their attack left 15 people dead and many hundreds injured.

For a couple of years we ran the night at The Britons Protection pub. We then received support from the Trade Union movement and the commemoration was held a hotel, which is now on the site where the massacre took place. That funding was short lived and we now hold the night at Bolton Socialist Club, a brilliant place where the spirit of resistance burns bright. It is an honour to perform there. Our evening and commemoration has no connection with any of the official Peterloo organisations, and Claire and I have never been invited to perform at any of their official functions.

This is a poem I was asked to write, and it bears no resemblance to the other, more famous poem.

As the cowards
Hid in shadows
On that fateful August day
Waiting for the order

To set upon their prey
Whilst the citizens of
Manchester
Gathered at
Petersfield
Calling for
Democracy
Determined not to
Yield
The leaders of the City
Had sealed the
People's fate
Ordering their yeomanry
To silence
The debate
With swords held high
Batons drawn
No mercy did they show
In Manchester
On that August day
Freedoms blood did flow
As the cowards sprung from
Shadows
The privileged smiled with
Delight
The citizens of our city
Did not refuse to fight
That day will be remembered
Forever in history
When people gathered at
Petersfield
Calling for

Freedom
Justice
Democracy

Why Speak Ill of The Dead?

When Margaret Thatcher died many of those on the left were criticised for celebrating. I personally could not celebrate but I could understand why many people did so. I don't believe in devils, but if they do exist Thatcher was mine. A vicious, nasty, bigot, who destroyed the social fabric of my country. In my stand up act I went on about Thatcher, and the damage she wrought, for many years. People used to tell me to let it go, that she was in the past. But she is not, even after her death she is still with us. Blair, Cameron, Osborne, Duncan Smith, Johnson are all her disciples.

No need to speak ill of the dead
Why would you need to
When her actions in life
Speak for themselves
The spite
The prejudice
Where there was peace
She took us to war

Where there was work
She created unemployment
Where there were wages
She created welfare

She saw value in conflict
In blind hatred
Her distaste for
Blue overalls and dirty hands

The enemy within
The miners
The commie unions
The council house scum

Her love of her friends
In the city
Of Reagan
Of Friedman
of Pol Pot
Of Apartheid

No
No need to speak ill
Of this woman

For
Her actions
In Life
Speak
For
Her

Bankers

In 2008 Capitalism in the western world hit the wall. What was genially termed a financial crisis was, in fact, the collapse of capitalism. The government of Britain bailed out British banks to the tune of, depending whom you believe, £500-750 billion. Some economists believe the country would have been better served by putting £10k into the bank account of every citizen. This would have allowed stretched households to go out and start spending, thus kick starting the economic recovery. Obviously, too simple a decision, and the government could not be seen to be giving poor people a hand out, handouts are reserved for the rich. If you don't believe me take a look at the Windsors.

The banks did get a bit of criticism, but as usual the poor got most of the blame. And it is the poor who are getting a kicking, from 2010, with the help of the Liberal Democrats, and now, in 2015, with a completely free hand, Gideon Osborne and his Thatcherite mates are literally killing the poor.

You took all our money
Let it go astray
Telling us it was safe with you
But it simply flew away
You spent it on things called
Futures
Commodities and
Derivatives
Dining out with your arrogance

Eating you own
Superlatives

You gambled it on hedge funds
Vulture Capitalist Deals
Then your gravy train
Hit the buffers
Coming off its greasy wheels
The end was almost in sight
For the greedy
Boys and Girls
Who used peoples lives
As if they were toys

Finished with your criminal sting
You nearly had your final fling
You had taken all the money
It simply blew away but
Feeding us with excuses and lies
You lived to fight another day

And now your are back
To where you were

To your bonuses
Greed and
Prosperity

Whilst the old and young alike
The sick and the poor
Are hit with
AUSTERITY.

Big Issue Seller

I live in Northenden, Wythenshawe, Manchester and at our small shopping centre, two or three times a week, a Big Issue seller stands outside the newsagents and trying to sell her copies of the magazine. She does not speak much English, but I always try to share a few words with her. One day she took some photographs from her bag and we had a stilted conversation. The photographs were of her grandchildren, in Bulgaria. I then showed her a picture of my granddaughter Amelie. This poem came out of that meeting.

My conversation with the old lady
Was somewhat stilted
She was from another country and
Did not speak English very well

But she pointed to my key ring
which held a picture of a little girl called
Amelie
She is my granddaughter

The lady stroked the picture
With her finger
Very beautiful she said
Grasping my hand she shouted

Gindobre
Gindobre

Then she turned away
Smiling at a
Passer by
Hoping to sell the a copy
Of her
Big Issue
The person passed by
Ignoring the
Old lady.

1984 Revisited

This is a poem I have only performed in public a couple of times. I am not sure why that is but intend to rectify that and perform it as often as I can. It is as relevant today as it was when I wrote it in 1992. I wrote it after attending a meeting, in Yorkshire addressed by Michael Heseltine. At the time he was President of something or other. He informed the meeting that the Tories were going to put the final nail in the coffin that was once the Mining Industry.

The meeting was addressed
By President Heseltine
In his blue suit
He looked sublime

What were we to learn on this fateful day
With so many problems in his way
He had agonised over this for ages
Things would happen in gradual stages

The mining industry was deep in trouble
The need for gas was about to double
Ten mines to go immediately
Twenty one more in
93

There was no other option
He told us so

30 Thousand Jobs
Would Have To Go
But there would be help
His government would
Pull out all the stops
Miners could set up
Their
One Man Butty Shops

His fellow Tories
Cared about
Miners
Lives
Their
Sons
Daughters
And
Their
Wives

But we could see through this charade
Decisions had already been made
Revenge would be extracted
For 73 and 84
The Tory government
Were about to
Even
The
Score.

In December 2015 the last, deep mine, coal mine in Britain, Kellingley Colliery, closed.

Burning Ambition

In 2011 a supposed friend of mine commented on the riots that had recently taken place. He said that the rioters were lacking in education, ambition and should be sent to prison. I, naturally disagreed with him, and wrote this poem for him. He did not read it, and we are no longer friends.

It is a long
Long way to travel
To get nothing in return
It is a lonely path to walk down
To watch
Ambitions burn

Whilst the criminals in the city
Spend their money without refrain
The homeless on
The littered streets
Seek shelter from the rain

And all the time
This happens
We are told progress
Is the goal
Not to question what
They tell us
Just to let them
Take our souls

Whilst the millionaires sit in
Parliament
Laughing at the
Poor
Throwing at them
The Bedroom Tax
Bringing loan sharks
To the door

From the
Ivory Towers
To the burnt out cars
Tax free havens
And Penny jars

It is long
Long way to travel
To get nothing in return
It is a lonely path to walk down
To watch
Ambitions burn.

Social Climbing

This is about some people who bought their council houses, or as it is now called social housing, whatever that term means. I am not completely opposed to anyone buying their home, but I believe that, for every council house sold one a new one should be built. But then again I believe that having a mortgage puts you into financial slavery, and the only people who really benefit are the banks. So I suppose I am against private property, after all I am a Marxist.

They were moving up the social scale
Buying their council house
Then in a few years time
They will put it up for sale

They will stop having dinner
Instead they'll take lunch
They won't have beer
They will have
Wine and Punch

They'll shop at
Sainsbury's
Out of town
When they get angry
They won't shout
They will just frown

They will give to charity
On their pay day
If Big Issue sellers stop them
They'll say go away

They will become
Middle class
A Cone
Or C 2

Then they can say

Us
Working Class
Certainly not
Are you?

Party for the Monarchs Sycophants

In 2012 Elizabeth Windsor visited Manchester to attend a civic function. Prior to this function my friend Claire Mooney had been employed to work with some young Manchester schoolchildren. Her job was to write a song and perform it, with the children, in front of the monarch. A lot of civic dignitaries were at the function. Whilst the children performed their song their monarch listened intently. The dignitaries didn't.

Drunk on power
And vanity
Ignoring the children
Who had been come
Te entertain them

The elected pimps
Filling their faces with
Free food
They talked and laughed
Whilst the children sang

Then
Summoned to meet their
Monarch

Their dignity
Abandoned

They formed
An orderly line
Waiting to
Kneel
To bow
To tug the
Forelock

Their power and
Their Vanity
Completely
Evaporated.

Eviction

This is a poem about a family who were evicted, by a labour council. This happened in the 1960's, but today in 2015 Labour councils are still evicting people.

Some people might have said
The garden was full of rubbish
The tatty three piece suite
The discarded clothes
Scattered on the grass
Alf Tupper looking up
From his comic

Trampled photographs
Covered in mud
Images hiding
As if from shame

The door of the house sealed
Preventing entry

And a family
Wondering
What the
Future
Holds.

Internet Dater

I accept that this is a very strange poem, and one I heave never had the bottle to perform, fully, in public. I wrote it after reading of the success rate of internet dating. The article said that 17% of marriages are between people who have met on the internet. I wondered what my profile might look like, if I ever decided to, or needed to, go onto an internet dating site.

Mature working class man
Seeks woman for friendship
Companionship or more
Am working class but not
Racist
Sexist
Homophobic
Violent drug taker or
Benefit Fraudster

Favourite places Whitby, Morecambe
Clevedon, and Wythenshawe
Varied music interests
Most admired authors
Marx, Galliano, Neruda
Mitchell, Fisk, Bennett
Tressel and Commons

Writes and performs poetry
Playwrite, screenwriter
And occasional and actor

Non-smoker
Non-drinker but is not
A miserable bastard

Politically left wing, Marxist, socialist
Pacifist, anti-monarchy republican
But, repeat, is not a miserable bastard

Good true friend
Considerate lover and particularly
Fond of experimenting
During lovemaking
Providing partner agrees

Enjoys holding partner after completion
Of said lovemaking

Anyone interested

Details attached.

Bombs r Us

In 2010 I read that Britain was at number one in the arms selling league, yes they do really have one of those. I decided to write this poem. Currently in 2016 we are at number 4.

We've got
Big bombs
Little bombs
Small bombs
Tiny bombs
Mini bombs
Thin bombs
Fat bombs
Dumb bombs
Quiet bombs
Silent bombs
Cluster bombs
Round Bombs
Square bombs
Long bombs
Short bombs
Flat bombs
Chap bpmbs
Dear bombs

Lots of bombs
Do you want some?

You're going
To
Get
Some.

Poem for Jean

On the 7th of December 1972 Jean McConville, a mother of ten children, was taken from her home in Belfast. She was taken by the local IRA and neighbours. On the previous night she had helped an injured and dying British soldier, who had been shot just outside her front door. She was taken from her home, put in the back of a car and taken to a beach, in County Louth.

Her shoes were taken from her and she was walked to a grave that had been dug by local IRA men. There she was shot in the back of the head. Before she was shot she was beaten and disfigured. The IRA returned her purse to her home, telling her children that Jean had gone to England. People have tried to smear Jean by saying that she was a low level spy for the British Government. No evidence has ever corroborated that accusation.

In 2003 a body was found on Shellinghill Beach, County Louth. It was the body of Jean McConville.

This is my poem about Jean.

They came in
Number
Eighteen of them
Fourteen men
Four women
They came for
One woman
A mighty woman
For Jean

They were neighbours
Friends
Comrades in
Catholicism
Brit haters
Unforgiving

Giving Jean
The bullets of
Righteousness

Jean
The mother
Jean
Full of Love
Full of compassion
Full of humanity

Jean
An example
To them
All.

Are We There Yet?

The whole world over, when children are taken on a trip by their parents, I suspect that they eventually ask their parents "are we nearly there yet". This poem is about two children who went on a journey with their parents, it wasn't a holiday journey. They were trying to escape war.

As they huddled next to their mother
Their flimsy craft rocking in the waves
Taking in sea water
Soaking them all
The youngest boy asked his mother
Are we nearly there yet
Showing him the lights on the
Nearby shore
She answered
Almost, we are almost there
What will happen to us
When we get there
The older boy asked
We will get a new home
A safe home
Your father will get
A new job
You and your brother
Will go to new schools
And we won't get bombed
Or shot at
She told him

Looking up at her he asked
What will happen if we don't
Get there
There was no reply.

Visit to a Benefit Office.

I had cause to visit a benefit office with a friend of mine. It was the middle of November and very cold. For anyone who has never been in one they are not very welcoming places. In fact they are quiet depressing, intimidating and unwelcoming, not only, I suspect, for those visiting but also for those who work there. The Tory government have introduced a system of sanctions which cut money off to already hard pressed individuals and families living in poverty. Up to March 2015, the latest figures I can get hold of, there were 587,000 people sanctioned.

At the desk next to us
A young man was arguing with
His adviser
This young man hadn't applied for the
Required number of jobs
Apparently, the adviser informed him
This had happened before
His benefit was to be suspended
The young man became angry
His rent was due

He needed to buy food
For his family
He needed to top up his
Gas and Electric
His needed to keep his children warm
He should have applied for the
Correct number of jobs
His adviser advised him
He had tried
There were no effing jobs
He screamed
The adviser pressed a button
Two G4S security guards ran to
The desk
They lifted the young man out of his
Chair
Rushed him to the door and
Took him outside
He swore and cursed them
My friends adviser looked at him
How are you today she enquired
My friend was to shocked
To reply.

Adverts Interrupted by Music

My favourite music is the music from the 60's. In Manchester there is a radio station that specialises in playing this type of music. Unfortunately, it is a commercial radio station and the music is constantly interrupted by adverts, or is it the other way round. I am a bit of an anorak and one day I monitored, for one hour, how long the adverts lasted. In that one hour the station played 34 minutes of music, 6 minutes of sky news and sport and 20 minutes of adverts. I wrote this poem after listening for one hour.

Terms and conditions
Always apply
Exclusions
Always apply
Offer not available in
Northern Ireland
Take only as
Directed
Always read the label
Credit subject to
Status
Your
Home
May
Be At
Risk
If

You
Do
Not
Keep
Up
Repayments
On
A
Mortgage
Or
Other
Loan
Secured
On
It.

The Red Doors and Coloured Bracelets

In January 2016 it was revealed that, in Middlesborough, a company sub-contracted by G4s, the governments favourite privateer, had housed asylum seekers and painted their doors red. This was done, the company said, so their workers could identify where the asylum seekers lived. Whilst in Cardiff, another privateer forced asylum seekers to wear brightly coloured wristbands. Those that refused to wear these wristbands were told they would not receive food or clothing vouchers. I wondered how this line of thinking went.

You can have blue, green, white
Brown, black or
Red
No I think we will give you
RED
Red doors are more distinctive
Easier to spot
Our drivers won't get confused when
They do a drive by
No need to get out of
Their vans
It can help the bigots
Too
The racists
The thugs
The fascists

With their
Eff off and
Go back home signs
They can throw eggs at
Your door
Bricks through your windows
They can spit and swear
At you
Insult your children
They can show you
A really
Warm Welcome to Britain
Oh!
And don't
Forget to
Wear your
Brightly
Coloured
Wristbands
So they can
Stop
You
In
The Street
And
Beat
You
Up.

We Are Not In This Together

The Tory chancellor Gideon Osborne has often told us all that, in the current climate of government driven austerity that "we are all in it together". All of us are suffering and that there is no alternative. Of course there are alternatives. It is just that the alternatives are beyond the idealogical scope of Osborne and his clique. As I put this book together the financial and banking sector are receiving higher bonuses than they were before they destroyed our economy. The rich are insulated, whilst zero hour contracts proliferate, public sector pay is frozen and local government services are privatised with abandon.

They say we are all in this together
It stops us banging on their door
They give tax cuts to the rich
And food banks to the poor
Bonuses to those who created
The mess
Wage cuts to the workers
Of the NHS
They hand out contracts
To tax-dodging privateers
Whilst the pleas of the needy
Are mocked and smeared
Their vandalism
Has no conscience
Knows no bounds

The victims shredded
Like the fox
Ripped apart by the hounds
The young, the old
The sick the poor
Are ridiculed and shamed
Derided
Humiliated
Laughed at and
Blamed
They say we are in this together
It's a lie they like to tell
They make the rich
Much richer
Whilst the poor
Can live in
Hell.

Gods

I wrote this poem shortly after George Bush and Tony Blair decided to invade Iraq in 2003. The invasion was, undoubtedly, a breach of international law, and caused the death of many hundreds of thousands of people. It caused the implosion of Iraq and set off a chain of events that have made the world a much more dangerous place than it was in 2003. Both Bush and Blair told us that, the night before the invasion started, they spoke to their respective gods. The pair of idiots asked their gods for guidance and their gods told them, as they often do, to go and kill innocent men, women and children. Neither Bush nor Blair has apologized for their action, and as far as I know, neither have their gods.

They spoke to
Their gods

Their Gods
Spoke back

Invoking them
To kill

It's odd
That
A God
Would

Do That
But as they say
Round our way

There's
Nowt
So
Strange
As
Gods.

Thursday Night Confession

My family lived in a council house in Woodhouse Park, Wythenshawe, Manchester. It was a lovely place to grow up. We lived near farms and open fields and could spend weekends and school summer holidays walking in the countryside, or playing in the air raid shelters of the small Ringway Airport, as it was then called. My dad was a royalist, and also a catholic .On the wall leading into our kitchen was a picture of the Pope, on the other was a picture of the Queen on the other. Going into the kitchen we had to cross ourselves, and coming back we had to bow. My way of getting out of this was to go through the living room door, and walking down the hallway through the door and into the kitchen. My dad got wind of this and one day, when I got home from school he had boarded up the hallway door. Every Thursday he would ask me if I was going to confession and I would always reply that I had nothing to confess. He would tell me to think of something on the way. So here is what I usually did.

On my way to confession
I'd call for my friend and
We'd go to Minsterley Parade
Asking one of the older boys to
Buy us a bottle of Woodpecker Cider
We'd sit in the doorways
Behind the shops
Drinking

Talking
Kissing
Laughing
Not knowing our futures
Would go in opposite
Directions

As we walked back home
We would hold hands
I'd wait at the end of her path
Watching her disappear indoors

And as I entered my house
My father would ask me
How many Hail Marys
I had to repeat

None I would answer
Good he shouted

Climbing into my bed
I'd rest my head on
The pillow
Close my eyes
Wondering if my
Fathers
God
Would punish
Me
For
My
Lies.

Royal Easter Parade

I wrote this poem after seeing, on the news, a caption of the Windsor family, and the rest of their clan, attending the annual Easter service on the Sandringham Estate in 2015.I was amazed, and somewhat saddened to see how many members of the public had turned out to see these people.

The women were dressed in
Pink, blue white and lemon
Some wore bonnets
There were Lady's Princesses
Countesses
And with them their
Queen
The men followed closely
Behind
In their dark
Hand made suits
All the clothes
We were told
Both for the men and
The women
Had been made by
Expensive
Exclusive
Designers
And
I added

To myself
Paid for
By
The Poor.

The Working Mum

In 2015 Margaret Windsor celebrated another birthday. At the celebrations was her great grandson and his wife Kate, better known as The Duchess of something or other. The Duchess had, six weeks before the celebrations given birth to a daughter, an event, in itself, a cause for great celebration. We were told, by the gushing media, that the Duchess was returning to work.I wrote this poem after watching the media spectacle.

The media praised her bravery
Returning to work
Six weeks after giving birth

Seeing the pictures of the Duchess
Being driven around
In an open top carriage

Smiling
Waving

The crowd waving back
Her new daughter being
Held by her nanny
On the Palace balcony

It made me think
If the definition
Of the word
Work
Had
Indeed
Been
Redefined.

How to End a Relationship With The Help of Roy Orbison Song Titles

This is a strange little poem that came to me early one morning when I woke up with a roy Orbison song in my head. I somehow, realised that his song titles were ideal material for a poem about splitting up. See what you think.

Claudette
I Drove All Night
From The Penny Arcade
Crying
Falling
Running Scared

Love Hurts
Blue Angel

It's Over
Pretty Woman

You Got It

Sweet
Dreams
Baby.

Modern Nursery Rhymes

I am including this little section in the book as a thank you to my granddaughter Amelie. A wonderful, happy, smiling, and caring bundle of humanity. In the first year reception class she told her teacher that her Gramps, that is me, was a poet and the teacher asked me to go in and see her. the teacher asked me if I would go into school and read some poetry to the children. I said that I would be honoured and told her to look at some of my stuff on the internet, which she obviously did, as she never got back to me. I never go the gig. It was a shame really because I had reworked some old nursery rhymes and I thought the children might have appreciated them. Here are a few of them.

Jack and Jill

Jack and Jill
Were sent up the hill
To Fetch a Pail of water
In the ensuing accident
Both Jack and Jill
Fell down the hill
And were injured
Their parents
Are being prosecuted
For child exploitation.

Humpty Dumpty

Humpty Dumpty sat on a wall
The maintenance of the wall
Had been outsourced to a for
Profit company and had been
Badly neglected
It collapsed
And Humpty Dumpty
Broke both of his legs
He is persuing
A personal injuries claim.

Little Jack Horner

Little Jack Horner

Mary, Mary

Mary, Mary

Sat in the corner
Eating his Christmas pie
He was rather quiet and
Didn't like eating in front
Of other children
He was referred to an
Educational psychologist
For assessment.

Was quite contrary
And as the Head Teacher
Was worried
About League tables
Mary was expelled
From the school.

Little Bo Peep

Little Bo Peep
Had lost her sheep
As it was the third
Time this had happened
She was instantly
Dismissed
For gross negligence.

Poor Tommy Tucker

Poor Tommy Tucker
Had to sing for his supper
His parents were on
Zero hour contracts
And had not worked for
A week.

Christmas Is a Coming

Christmas is a coming
Geese are getting fat
Please put a pound
In the old mans hat
If you haven't got a pound
Fifty pence will do
If you haven't got either
It's the food bank for you.

The Grand Old Duke of York

The grand old Duke of York
Had ten thousand men
He marched them up to the
Top of the hill
Where they mutinied
Shooting him in the head.

We (The working Class)

This is a poem about being working class, people who generally work hard for little reward, and are usually the poorest in our very unequal society. Over the past half a century politicians of all parties have consistently presented our country as a classless society. They have been clever at manipulating us, as citizens, by concentrating societal arguments around ethnicity. Being working class means suffering discrimination, no matter what ethnicity we may be from. It has been said to me, on more than one occasion, that I have a chip on my shoulder. This is a phrase who's origins are disputed, but is generally thought to mean that a grievance is carried by the person who is said to carry the chip. When I am asked if I do have a chip on my shoulder I reply that I do not have one, but two, and they are big ones.

We've been schooled
We've been fooled
We've been preached at
We've been screeched at
We've been drilled
We've been killed

We've been packed
We've been sacked
We've been kicked
We've been pricked
We've been shipped
We've been whipped

We've been taught to bow
We've been made to cow
We've been patronized
We've been criminalized
We've been demonized
We've been socialized

We've been laughed at
We've been scoffed at
We've been lumped
We've been dumped

We've been screened
We've been cleaned
We've been inspected
We've been rejected

We've been taught to brawl
We've been ordered to crawl
We've been asked to prey
We've been put away
We've been sent to war
We've been shown the door

We've been on TV
We've been you and me
How utterly crass
We've been
WORKING
CLASS.

For Benny Rothman

On April 24th 1932 the mass trespass of Kinder Scout took place. One of its leaders was a Manchester man named Benny Rothman. Benny was political activist, a socialist and communist, and also involved in trade union activities and heavily in community work. On April 24th Benny and other activists walked to the top of Kinder Scout, meeting another group of walkers there. They were confronted by large numbers of police and armed gamekeepers. They were prevented from walking to the top of Kinder Scout, arrested, charged and taken to court. Benny and some other activists were imprisoned.

Every April the Morning Star, the only socialist daily newspaper in Europ,e organises a trek up Kinder Scout in honour of Benny Rothman and the group of trespassers. I have been asked on two occasions, by the Morning Star, to perform poetry at the top of Kinder Scout. Here are two of the poems I wrote for those occasions.

No man has the tight
To own mountains
Yet we know that many
Still do
They own valleys, rivers
Cities and towns
Islands and palaces too

So let us erase the memory
Of the idle rich

Their lazy indolent ways
This land should be shared
By everyone
For now and the
Rest of days

Demolish the walls
The keep out signs
Stop the arrests
Refund the fines
Let everyone walk
Without favour or fear
Every day of
Every year

No family has the right
To own mountains
That is clear for all to see
This land can be shared
By everyone
You
You
You
And
Me.

Never Afraid

This is another poem I performed at the top of Kinder Scout IN MEMORY OF Benny Rothmand and the Kinder Scout Trespassers.

Never afraid to confront
Injustice
Avarice
Prejudice and Ignorance
The man named
Benny Rothman
A hero without a doubt
Opened up
The Dark Peaks
Bleaklow and
Kinder Scout
What is good enough for
The rich
Is good enough for us
He would say
That is why we can
Walk there today

Unwilling to accept
The signs that read
Private Land
No trespassers
Public keep out

Unafraid of what he faced
Defying the dogs
The guns
The police
The courts
So we could walk freely
Upon the open space

He fought the toffs
The lickspittle gamekeepers
Holding out their hands
For the crumbs off their
Lords table

The man named
Benny Rothman
A hero without a doubt
Opened up the
Dark Peaks
Bleaklow and
Kinder Scout.

Let's Have a Revolution for Fun

This is a poem that was inspired by a work by D H Lawrence. It is a poem that I have recently started performing again. I enjoy performing it and it usually gets a good reception. Some of my friends tell me it is a naïve poem.

Let's have a revolution
Without violence or malice
We could have the launch
At Buckingham Palace
Let's have politicians
Eating clichés and lies
Invade their hypocrisies
With soft custard pies
Let's get rid of borders
That keep the poor at bay
Let's have
You Are Welcome
Signs
We hope you will stay

Let's stop making warplanes
Tanks and guns
Teach humanity
To our
Daughters and sons
Let age old enemies
Turn a new page

Let love and kindness
Replace
Hatred and rage

Let everyone share
In the wealth that is made
Let's have a regular
Happy parade

Let's have a revolution
Every place everywhere
Let's have a revolution
To show we all care

Let's have a revolution
Without violence or malice
Let's have the launch
At a
People's Palace.

The Lights Never Go Out at Buckingham Palace

This poem cam about after I read that the lights at Buckingham Palace are never switched off. As most of us know that is where Elizabeth Windsor and her husband Philip live. They live there with hundreds of servants.

They never turn the
Lights out at
Buckingham Palace

Bur there again
The people who
Live there
Never have to
Pay
The Bill.

Come to Sellafield

When it comes to nuclear energy successive governments have repeatedly ignored the views of the public, who rightly or wrongly, are not convinced that a product, once it has been used, needs to be encased in concrete, entombed in a lead lined box, buried three miles underground and left alone for 10,000 years, is safe. I wrote this poem after I heard a local commercial radio advertising the advantages of taking a trip to the visitors centre at theSellafield nuclear re-processing plant at in Cumbria.

Come to Sellafield
It's a great day out
You can feel
You can touch
You can mess about

Come to Sellafield
Have some fun
You can watch
Our
Plutonium
Production run

Come to Sellafield
See the Dead Sea
There's lots to do
For you and me

Come to Sellafield
It's such a great sight
We have cows and sheep
That glow in the night

Come to Sellafield It's really a must
We can show you
A local
Cancer Cluster

Come to Sellafield
It's Hyperactive
It's Interactive
It's Superactive

And hey
It's
RADIOACTIVE.

Two Lives

Elizabeth Windsor, also known as The Queen of Great Britain and the Commonwealth, celebrated her 90th Birthday towards the end of April 2016.The media, and many parts of the country went into an orgy of sycophantic reverence. There will also be another celebration later in the year. These will be called the official birthday celebrations, and we can expect the same level of hero worship when they take place. At about the same time as the nation was on its knees to Mrs Windsor I read a story about another 90 year old lady, who was found in her flat, had almost died from malnutrition and was only saved by a neighbour who had not seen her for a few weeks.

One loved
One ignored

One cared for
One unsure

A life of pleasure
A life of toil

A hand in a glove
A hand in soil

Too rich to care
Too poor to share

Too sheltered to worry
Too sad to hurry

Two lives soon
Will end

One loved
By a nation

One
Without
A friend.

Elephants, Rhinos and Robin Hood

This little poem came out of a conversation I, and my wife Babs, had with our wonderful granddaughter Amelie. She is an intelligent, thoughtful ,considerat,e fun loving girl and we talk about all kinds of things, the Russian revolution, the monarchy, religion, and we play some wonderful games.

Amelie told us about the Elephants
And the Rhinos
Slaughtered for their tusks
Their bodies left to rot
Whilst the tusks were made
Into jewellery and ornaments

She said it was the fault of
Rich people
Greedy people
Cruel people

She informed us that Elephants
Were caring and beautiful
That Rhinos were proud
And noble

Then she paused
And asked us if we could play
Robin Hood.

I Have a Dream

I have a dream is dedicated to the memory of Miss Daisy Speedwell, who was locked up, in a mental health facility, (actually it was an asylum), or over 40 years. She was locked up for being, as a child, too happy. As a young girl she used to whistle and sing tunes. People thought that she was mad and she was locked up. When she was released, despite all that had happened to her, she was still happy, but slightly bitter. She said that all she had ever wanted to do was make people happy and full of love.

The poem contains a quote from Martin Luther King and some of the titles of some of my favourite songs. I have been told, on a number of occasions that I need to add some new song titles. Why should I?

I have a dream
I believe in love
Love is all you need
I am going to record
My favourite love songs
Send them to the
Leaders of the world
Make the listen to
This old heart of mine
Join the
Caravan of love
Get on board
The love train

Tell them
Love is in the air
Of the
Power of love
The eternal flame
The glory of love
Ask them to
Unchain the melody
Be for real

Love the fascist
Love the racist
Love the bigot
Love the enemy
Love the neighbour
Love all
Hate none

I have a dream
Love is all you need
Love is all you need
Love is all you need.